ALFRED A. KNOPF
1915 · 100 YEARS · 2015

He, She and It

Summer People

Gone to Soldiers

Fly Away Home

Braided Lives (republished 2013)

Vida (republished 2011)

The High Cost of Living

Woman on the Edge of Time

Small Changes

Dance the Eagle to Sleep (republished 2012)

Small Changes

OTHER

The Cost of Lunch, Etc. (A collection of short stories)

Pesach for the Rest of Us

So You Want to Write: How to Master the Craft of Writing Fiction and
Personal Narrative (with Ira Wood), 1st & 2nd editions

The Last White Class: A Play (with Ira Wood)

Sleeping with Cats: A Memoir

Parti-Colored Blocks for a Quilt (Essays)

Early Ripening: American Women's Poetry Now (Anthology)

MADE IN DETROIT

MADE IN DETROIT

Poems

MARGE PIERCY

ALFRED A. KNOPF   NEW YORK   2015

THIS IS A BORZOI BOOK
PUBLISHED BY ALFRED A. KNOPF

Copyright 2015 © by Marge Piercy

www.aaknopf.com/poetry

Knopf, Borzoi Books, and the colophon are registered
trademarks of Random House LLC.

Original publication information for the previously published poems
included in this collection is located on page 169.

Library of Congress Cataloging-in-Publication Data
Piercy, Marge.
[Poems. Selections]
Made in Detroit : poems / Marge Piercy. — First edition.
pages ; cm
"This is a Borzoi Book."
ISBN 978-0-385-35388-5 (hardcover) — ISBN 978-0-385-35389-2 (ebook)
I. Title.
PS8566.I4A6 2015
811'.54—dc23
2014026429

Jacket image: Library, courtesy of Lori Nix and Kathleen Gerber
Jacket design by Abby Weintraub

Manufactured in the United States of America
Published March 31, 2015
Second Printing May 2015

CONTENTS

I   Made in Detroit

II Ignorance bigger than the moon

III The poor are no longer with us

IV   Working at it

VI Looking back in utter confusion

I

Made in Detroit

Made in Detroit

My first lessons were kisses and a hammer.
I was fed with mother's milk and rat poison.
I learned to walk on a tightrope over a pit
where snakes' warnings were my rattles.

The night I was born the sky burned red
over Detroit and sirens sharpened their knives.
The elms made tents of solace over grimy
streets and alley cats purred me to sleep.

I dived into books and their fables
closed over my head and hid me.
Libraries were my cathedrals. Librarians
my priests promising salvation.

I was formed by beating like a black
smith's sword, and my edge is still
sharp enough to cut both you and me.
I sought love in dark and dusty corners

and sometimes I even found it
however briefly. Every harsh, every
tender word entered my flesh and lives
there still, bacteria inside my gut.

I suckled Detroit's steel tits. When
I escaped to college I carried it with
me, shadow and voice, pressure
that hardened me to coal and flame.

The frontroom

In the tiny livingroom of my parents' house
that my mother, brought up in tenements
always called the frontroom, stood
a maroon couch with rough itchy
upholstery that marked my tender
thighs if ever I sat on it.

On every surface, wooden shoes,
Eiffel tower, leather teepee,
ceramic dolls in costume—
souvenirs of places they had
gone or she wished she had.
She hated an empty space.

Emptiness meant poverty. With
money she would have collected
paintings, objets d'art which these
were to her, emblems of times away
from our asbestos shack where she
imagined a richer life. Out of library

books, images like genii rose murmuring
your wish is my etcetera. But she
commanded nothing except my child
labor rubbing, scrubbing what could
never be clean, as factory soot
drifted down like ebony snow.

Detroit, February 1943

When there was wind, it found
every crack and chink in the walls.
On winter mornings, the windows
were etched with landscapes
of frost eerie and delicate.

Rising from my cold bed
into the cold room, my clothes
laid out for school stiff, rustling
with cold, I would run to stand
over the hot air register, hoping

the furnace had been fed coal.
My father's cigarette cough
rattled from their room.
I smelled oatmeal. Once we
ate it for three weeks of hunger.

My clothes were shaped
by other bodies, my books
had corners turned down,
notes I could not read.
Rummage sales were our malls.

My mother fed birds, talking
with them as they flew to perch
near her, leftovers, stale bread,
crumbs. We too survived
on what no one else wanted.

Things that will never happen here again

I remember hauling carpets out to the clothes
lines in the yard and knocking the dust out
in great cough-making clouds with wire
carpet beaters like diagrams of cellos.

Defrosting the refrigerator required much
boiling of water on the stove and flat pans
into which fingers of ice fell. Every five
minutes water cooled and needed refilling.

The coal truck came and down the chute
into the coal bin the black rocks
clattered and thundered. The floors
upstairs shook in a local quake.

The furnace with its many arms lurked
in the basement and every few days
clinkers must be removed, often still
smoking, and ashes hauled out.

During the war we collected cans
and stomped them underfoot, handing
them in. We bundled newspapers,
magazines for distant factories.

I miss none of this. They were chores
not pleasures, but still I remember
and my age hangs on me like icicles
that bear down the branches of pine.

Detroit fauna

I am old enough to remember the sad
horses that pulled open-sided carts
loaded with vegetables and fruit,
the knife sharpener's whirring stone,
the rag man in the alley, the closed
dripping wagon of the ice man.

They were always brown or grey.
They walked and stopped, walked
on then stopped, their heads bowed
under the burden of dragging
heaviness across hot asphalt, day
after day for what scant reward?

Police horses are bigger and glossy.
I never pitied them when they
charged us. They were the enemy
grim as war horses that snuffled
fire as they trampled the infantry,
stallions bred to die on pikes.

Even the glass bottles of milk
were carried to our breakfasts
by horses. The photographer
went house to house with his pony
black and white spotted, adorned
with bells, but the working stiffs

never had tails plaited or manes
brushed out. I spoke to them
and their red-rimmed eyes would
turn to me. Then off they would clop
clop in the harness we were
each supposed to grow into.

Family vacation to Yellowstone

I kept a diary my twelfth summer
when we took our first long trip
since before the war. I wrote up
every meal, a skinny pale blue
child with sprouting sore breasts
I slumped to hide. Always hungry.

"For lunch at a place called The
Green Frog I had fried cat
fish, corn bread and mashed
potatoes. For dessert I ate
strawberry ice cream!! It
was all very delicious."

Besides every piece of food
I mentioned only animals. An owl
tethered at a restaurant in Frankenmuth
Michigan, an owl called Jerry
a woman bathed and dried.
I described a horse who whinnied

at me over a fence in Wyoming.
I lovingly listed cattle and eagles,
antelope and elk, bison. Animals
I trusted as frightened children

do. My father's temper. My mother's
anger. I would have run away

with a wolf pack. In Yellowstone
I decided my future as a ranger.
I would live among pine trees
and follow bison through
the tall grass. We met a man
who lived up in a fire tower

and I wanted to become him.
I wanted a tower not like Rapunzel
to coax a lover to climb,
but to rise up and hide, high
above smoky buzzing Detroit
streets, the tiny asbestos shack

thrumming with unpaid bills
and the marriage of the cat
and dog with their unloved
offspring thin as a knife—
all of us with edges that
made each other bleed.

The rented lakes of my childhood

I remember the lakes of my Michigan
childhood. Here they are called ponds.
Lakes belonged to summer, two-week
vacations that my father was granted by
Westinghouse when we rented some cabin.

Never mind the dishes with spiderweb
cracks, the crooked aluminum sauce
pans, the crusted black frying pans.
Never mind the mattresses shaped
like the letter V. Old jangling springs.

Moldy bathrooms. Low ceilings
that leaked. The lakes were mysteries
of sand and filmy weeds and minnows
flickering through my fingers. I rowed
into freedom. Alone on the water

that freckled into small ripples,
that raised its hackles in storms,
that lay glassy at twilight reflecting
the sunset then sucking up the dark,
I was unobserved as the quiet doe

coming with her fauns to drink
on the opposite shore. I let the row-
boat drift as the current pleased, lying

faceup like a photographer's plate
the rising moon turned to a ghost.

And though the voices called me
back to the rented space we shared
I was sure I left my real self there—
a tiny black pupil in the immense
eye of a silver pool of silence.

Thirteen

The girl was closed on herself
tight as a winter bud on a sugar
maple, protecting what lay within.

She imagined herself a foundling—
secret offspring of some kind, rich
parents, but the mirror contradicted.

Her shoulders hunched over newly
sprouted breasts sour as crab
apples and as hard to the touch.

Her shoulders hunched over dreams
cradled within like wet birds
just broken free of the eggshell.

Her hair fell over her face, a black
veil hiding her staring eyes that
sought distance and strange places.

Within her will was tempered
like fine steel by every rebuke
every insult, every beating—

a weapon she honed in dreams,
in solitude till its double-bladed
ax could knock a hole in any wall.

She held forth

The neighborhood women
always came to my mother,
never she to them. Salesmen,
solicitors, invited couples
rang the front doorbell.

The women came to the grade
door in the yard, following
the cracked cement walk around
the asbestos siding, then knocking,
calling, *Bert,* my mother's full name,

or softening it to *Bertie! Bertie. . . .*
She would summon them up
the steps to the kitchen past
rows of shoe polish and garden
tools on the shelf to the side

into the kitchen with its worn
yellow linoleum and oilcloth
covered table. She would serve
tea or lemonade and they would
hold out their palms to her,

hands cracked or water-softened
with labor, a few manicured,
some twisted with arthritis
to gnarled burls. She would study
their palms and then she would

tell them what was and would
be, what to fear and what to
avoid and sometime promises
of windfalls or even love.
Again and again they came

as if she could change their
futures. Sometimes she'd give
them folk remedies for ailments
they would not tell the doctor
or hadn't the money for him.

By four she'd shoo them out
because what *she* feared might
come at any moment, my father's
bolt of temper, acid mockery.
She wiped the table and set it.

The scent of apple cake

My mother cooked as drudgery
the same fifteen dishes round
and round like a donkey bound
to a millstone grinding dust.

My mother baked as a dance,
the flour falling from the sifter
in a rain of fine white pollen.
The sugar was sweet snow.

The dough beneath her palms
was the warm flesh of a baby
when they were all hers before
their wills sprouted like mushrooms.

Cookies she formed in rows
on the baking sheets, oatmeal,
molasses, lemon, chocolate chip,
delights anyone could love.

Love was in short supply,
but pies were obedient to her
command of their pastry, crisp
holding the sweetness within.

Desserts were her reward for endless
cleaning in the acid yellow cloud

of Detroit, begging dollars from
my father, mending, darning, bleaching.

In the oven she made sweetness
where otherwise there was none.

By the river of Detroit

By the river of Detroit
I did not weep but sulked
and stormed and bit hard
into anything sweet or
succulent I came upon.

My adolescence was grey,
fogged in with prohibitions
My lust was a stunted gnarled
tree that bore onions—
fruit tough as horse chestnuts.

I would have run off
with any stranger who asked.
I beat against the walls
of my room like a rabid
bat and in my diary

I confessed madness
and amorphous sins I
could find no partner
to share. I praised suicide
and went on crossly living.

I understand those girls
who hang themselves in closets.
Wait, I want to whisper,

then run and hide and run
out of that mangling time

only jocks, pink girls and idiots
think wonderful. Get
thee to a place where
other freaks and geeks
flourish and join the dance.

The street that was

I walk down the same street
as always past the same brick
apartment house with the marble
step, past the scabby clapboard
the owners never bother to paint.

There's the porch with plastic
geraniums, there's the woman
with the goiter peering through
lace curtains hoping to spy
an affair or theft ripe for gossip.

There's the house where upstairs
Dolly's dressinggown caught fire
at the stove. I watched firemen
carrying her out. Her dog
went whimpering after them,

was left at the curb. How
could I know that cloudy morning
was the last? In my mind
those houses still stand peeling,
lace curtained, everything stuck

in a diorama of working-class
fifties while I am the bird
that has flown east, south, west,
across the ocean and back
to some place but never there.

City bleeding

Oh my city of origin, city who taught
me about class and class warfare,
who informed me how to survive
on your ashgrey burning streets
when as a Jew I was not white yet,
easy among friends of all colors,

how you have been plundered
and picked to pitted rusting bones.
Around you squat suburbs that never
saw a rat or woke to sirens cutting
machete wounds through the night,
whose lush lawns were fertilized

by your jobs exported to China,
by bodies of desperate murders.
This sand is fertile. Two years
after fire leaves a blackened pit
bushes are already sprouting
among blue and gold wildflowers.

In blocks of zombie houses, crack
houses, walls of gang graffiti,
where packs of wild dogs turn back

to wolves and the police never come,
people still try with little help
to remake community, to reach up

and out of rubble into some venue
of light, of warmth, of dignity, into
whatever peace they imagine. Out
of ruins eerie in their torn decay
where people lived, worked, dreamed
something yet begins to rise and grow.

Mehitabel & me

My junior year of college I played
a record of Archy and Mehitabel
dozens of times. I knew all
the alley cat's lyrics. I was sure
I was her, poor, ill dressed

in a crowd of cashmere virgins
already had several lovers, a self
administered abortion, working
three jobs to stay in school, a poet
no one but myself took seriously.

Poets weren't street sluts from Detroit.
I dressed all in black, turtleneck,
black jeans, heavy eye makeup.
Black doesn't show dirt. Not
infrequently I was hungry. No

winter coat so I shook in the wind
like a tree stripped of leaves. I drank
whiskey as poets were supposed to.
While good girls were locked in dorm
rooms, I wandered, partied, got laid.

I expected little but trouble. Yet
I wrote and began to win prizes.
I still expected to die young, poor

and unmourned, but with a grin,
a wry joke, in love with lady irony.

I'm middle class now and loved
in a funky house I own with money
from writing I saved to buy. I take
in cats. I drink good wine and my
own cooking. I'm still surprised.

What my mother gave me

Oh mother running an old vacuum
back and forth on a threadbare rug
while my retired father supervised—

if you had the wings of the robins,
jays and cardinals you fed daily
out of the window you'd have flown

to some garden of peach trees
and peonies, a garden of roses
and tomatoes red as lipstick:

a garden where you could sit
on cushions and cats would circle
your feet purring your Hebrew name.

Oh mother your ashes feed
wisteria rampant as your dreams
that withered to salt on your pillow.

You dreamed of love that would
bathe you in radiance and got
the lye of contempt in your throat.

Who ever looked past the faded

housedresses limp on your breasts
to the child still hungering within?

That hunger haunts me staring
from eyes of women in the subway,
women in the unemployment office

women cowering under a rain of fire,
women bruised in emergency rooms.
You are my first muse. Your pain

is my ink. I am the daughter
of your fierce lonely cry: poverty
of respect, of love, of hope.

Our neverending entanglement

How long do we mourn our mothers?
Unfinished business. Unspoken
sentences that burn on the night.
Tangled thickets of stymied
love. Steps worn smooth
with scrubbing, never to be
climbed again.

We mourn our mothers till
we ourselves are out
of breath. That umbilical
cord between us, never
really cut no matter how
hard we tried in adolescence
to sever it.

Once there was warm
milk in a sweet stream
Once there was a brush
stroking through my long

hair. Once there was a lap.
Once there was a slap.
Shards of glass.

Will anyone ever come
as close or push as
hard? As we age we
see your face mirrored.
Your diseases weaken
us. Your silences haunt,
your stories echo.

We feared becoming our
mothers yet when we were
not you, we felt guilty.
You made us even when
you hated the results
for you opened your fists
and off we flew.

Ashes in their places

I put my mother into the garden
I put my father into the sea.
Without her he complained of the fish,
the cold salt water too rough.

Without him she became
a climbing rose and rushed
up the arbor, twining, bursting
into lush pink perfumed bloom.

Gradually he swept out toward
tankers, container vessels,
a passing destroyer. He liked
their engines. He understood

engines. Women were too
emotional. He had to scare them
quiet, but ships had a purpose.
When my cats died, she welcomed

them into her bed. When I
picked her roses, she crooned
to me. *I don't need lullabies,*
I said. *Everybody nowadays*

needs more sleep, she whispered.
I sleep much better here.

.

II

Ignorance bigger than the moon

January orders

Snow turns the garden white
as soap powder with blue shadows
striping the abraded furrows.

Even the pebbles in the drive
glint with ice, but inside bent
over an old coffeetable dragged

from the shed, we peruse out loud
seed catalogs, debate inflated
verbiage on tomatoes, peppers,

lettuce. What glorious photos
of polished perfect eggplants,
of even orthodontist rows

of corn kernels like model's teeth.
Everything is super early, tasty
and resistant to all plagues

known to the studious gardener.
Surely we'll be buried in squash.
No cuke beetles will nibble on us.

Our harvests are blessed in advance

by glossy pages of promises
that seduce us to order too much

of what will endure weeks of rain,
a month or two of drought, beetles,
chipmunks, deer, hail and hurricane

before we plop it into our mouths,
the freezer, the frying pan, or, alas,
rotting into the compost pile.

We have come through

The faintest paring of moon rises
tonight just barely silvering the mounds
of snow that used to be cars, fenceposts,
bushes, a wheelbarrow perhaps.

The world has become anonymous
everything painted and padded white
the road the same as the field it ran
through, the tallest bushes bowed.

We are stuck here without exit,
barricaded into silence. The wind
that pelted the windows opaque
that broke the white fir at its base

that pushed tiny crystal knives
sideways and froze birds on their
perches has slunk away to sea
where it harries ships and gulls.

We will dig out. We will clean up.
A plow will come and recreate
the asphalt road. Town will awake
into lights and people will meet

and ask, how was the storm for you?
How long were you without power?
Trees down? We the survivors
cautiously examine our luck.

How I gained respect for night herons

It was shortly after dawn.
We were passing an inn closed
for the season when I yelled
"Stop!" I've often heard night
herons squawking hoarsely

or the screech of a murder
victim deep in the marsh.
Seldom do I see them. They
hunch on dead trees like old
men in cold weather. But

this black crowned night heron
was standing in the driveway
of the inn engaged in mortal
battle with a five-foot-long
water snake twisting, striking

him whose impulse was to fly off
from us but here was a huge meal.
Breeding season. A nest of young
gaping for food. It stood its ground
the snake grasped in its beak

shaking it, biting into it, lashed
by the long muscular tail. We
crept close enough to see

the heron's bright red eyes
polished buttons glinting fiercely.

It was an epic battle, Laocoon
encircled by serpents, but here
he was winning, barely. Not
a commanding figure, squatter than
most herons, drably plumaged

not the sort of bird we'd cast
as hero, but he wouldn't give up.
At last he cut through the spine
and slowly overloaded made his
way flying low toward his home.

Remnants still visible

Robins migrate, all schoolchildren
learn but here on the Cape, every
winter a flock forms and stays,
long frigid months after their
compatriots have flown south.

They live deep in the woods on
hips and berries wizened by cold.
Sometimes they appear here
among the feeder birds, one
or two almost outcasts.

Off Alaska when humpback whales
leave in fall as the waters freeze
and the world turns white, heading
for mating grounds off Hawaii
and Mexico, certain whales remain.

What makes a creature stay when
almost all of its kind have moved on?
In burned-out areas of Detroit,
you'll notice one house still wears
curtains, a bike locked to the porch.

Sometimes in the suburbs among
tract houses with carpets of grass
one farmhouse lurks, maybe even

with a barn. I imagine its owner
grey and stubborn, still growing

the best tomatoes for miles, refusing
to plant inedible grass, fighting
neighbors about her chickens,
a rooster who crows at four,
her clothesline a flag of defiance.

The constant exchange

The ocean gives; the ocean takes away.
I walked the old coast guard road many
afternoons, just behind the last dune.
Storms slammed it down, the waves
ate it entire with the whole front dune.

I remember a summer house where we
dined with friends several times, remember
how one winter it hung awkwardly half
over the cliff and then it was gone.
A lone pipe remained for another year.

On old maps the hills on the Bay called
Griffin Island, Bound Brook Island were
just that and now solid land. Only
marshes of reed and sedge seethe
and ebb where tall ships docked.

The sea is restless and greedy. It mocks
the summer people with their million
dollar houses with huge decks, vast
glass, chews them up to splinters, then
totes their flotsam away to dump on some

beach fifty miles distant as grey drift-
wood. Every spring we visit town beaches

to find the parking lot broken to rough
chunks, the stairs washed away. Ocean
takes no guff from us tiny creatures

but we get ours back by poisoning it.

May opens wide

The rain that came down last night
in sheets of shaken foil while thunder
trundled over the Bay and crooked
spears of lightning splintered trees

is rising now up stalks, lengthening
leaves that wave their new bright
banners tender as petals, seventeen
shades of green pushing into sun.

The soil feels sweet in my hands
as I push little marigolds in.
Bumblebees stir in the sour cherry
blossoms floating like pieces of moon

down to the red tulips beneath
the smooth barked tree where a red
squirrel chatters at my rescued tabby
who eyes him like a plate of lunch.

Wisteria can pull down a house

The wisteria means to creep over the world.
Every day its long tendrils wave in the breeze,
seize the bench under its arbor, weave
round the garden fence obstructing
the path. Its arbor's long outgrown.

Such avidity. Such greed for dominance.
It has already killed the Siberian irises
it shadowed, stealing all their sun.
Should I admire or resent? Neither.
I go out with loppers and hack and hack.

If it could, it would twine around my neck
like a python; like an angry giant squid
it would pull me into a strangling embrace.
I will grow back, it swears, and outlive you.
Its vigor outdoes mine. It will succeed.

June 15th, 8 p.m.

The evening comes slowly over us,
over the cardinal and the wren still
feeding, over the swallows suddenly
swooping to snatch up mosquitoes

over the marsh where the green
sedge lately has a tawny tinge
over two yearlings bending long
necks to nibble hillock bushes

finally separate from their doe
mother. A late hawk is circling
against the sky streaked lavender.
The breeze has quieted, vanished

into leaves that still stir a bit
like a cat turning round before
sleep. Distantly a car passes
and is gone. Night gradually

unrolls from the east where
the ocean slides up and down
the sand leaving seaweed tassels:
a perfect world for moments.

Hard rain and potent thunder

An elephant herd of storm clouds
trample overhead. The air vibrates
electrically. The wind is rough
as hide scraping my face.

Longhaired rain occludes the pines.
This storm seems personal. We
crouch under the weight of the laden
air, feeling silly to be afraid.

Water comes sideways attacking
the shingles. The skylight drips.
We feel trapped in high surf
and buffeted. When the nickel

moon finally appears dripping
we are as relieved as if an in-
truder had threatened us and
then walked off with a shrug.

Ignorance bigger than the moon

A fly is knocking itself senseless
against the pane. That is, if a fly's
brain is in its head. Lobsters
do not lodge the center
of their nervous system there

if one is to think of a fly
as an inconvenient lobster,
arthropods all. I've been reading
about the ways plants commu-
nicate by chemicals, wondering

if a tomato plant minds more
if a chipmunk bites into its fruit
or if I pick its ripe globes.
A moth is trapped between
the screen and closed window.

If I had super hearing like
a vampire, would I be bothered
by its screaming? The world
surrounds me with small
mysteries. How ignorant I am.

Or bigger ones. Does a tree
suffer when it's chopped

down? Is earth weary of us
who poison it? Is she calling
even now to sister meteors?

I go through my muddled life
like a pebble pushed by currents
I don't acknowledge. I notice
perhaps a hundredth of what
swarms about me on every side.

Yet if I could feel it all, hear
every whisper or cry, notice
all the faces in a crowded street,
would I really be wiser? or only
more confused, dumb and deafened.

Little house with no door

For decades it stood in the oak woods
not on any road but found only
by an old path half grown over:
a one-room house with no door

left to shut anyone out, windows
long bereft of glass, a few holes
in the roof where sky poked through.
I met a lover there one summer.

I had a tense political argument
with a fugitive there. A woman
who'd left her rich husband
for poverty spent two months

camped in it. Raccoons explored,
squirrels bopped in and out.
Rain sidled through the floor.
Once in a while someone or other

made repairs till bloated houses
of summer people blocked access
and gradually it knelt down into
the forest floor and collapsed

taking all that history with it.
I never knew who built it way

into the woods, perhaps a hunter,
perhaps a hermit. Perhaps a ghost.

Still it sheltered with its ravaged
roof teenagers drinking and fucking,
romance and the end of it, and for whoever
most needed it, privacy, maybe peace.

There were no mountains in Detroit [haibun]

When I was a child, my parents would drive to Ebensburg, Pennsylvania, in soft coal country in the Appalachians a couple of times a year, often just as summer was ending—before school started. My father had grown up there and his sisters still lived in the narrow house resembling a red brick tombstone that stretched back from the highway where trucks groaned up the steep hill all night making me think of dinosaurs in books. I was never comfortable there, feeling alien, feeling very Jewish and judged, but I loved the mountains. When we left for home with my father at the wheel, early in the morning to reach Detroit the same day, there would always be fog, low clouds along the twisty highway. My father drove fast past the company coal towns, past the rock faces often stained with rust, the abandoned coke ovens, the mine entrances that looked foreboding where my uncle and second and third cousins worked under the mountains, the occasional stream dashing itself against rocks, the dark forests where my uncle Zimmy hunted deer on Sundays.

> A cloud rests white on
> a mountain's shoulder: snow's hand
> on the back of fall.

But soon there will be none

The garden is oppressing me
with its rich bounty that is so
many debts to be paid. Tomatoes
I tucked into the ground up
to their hips in late April, little
miniature trees only so tall
as the space from wrist
to elbow, now they are shaggy
giants that tower over me.
They are laden like bizarre
Christmas trees with red,
with purple, yellow, pink,
orange and maroon fruit, all
to be gathered, heavy as
a small child in the basket.
All to be spread on platters
in the diningroom where we
dine with elbows tucked
in the two square feet they
leave us. Can, make into sauce,
Italian, hot, simple. Shove in
the dehydrator to make sweet
dry slices like candy. Freeze
as soup. Cook into chutney.
Fill the bathtub and jump in.
Force them down the cats.
And eat and eat and eat

and eat and eat. I dream
they are crawling through
the window into my bed
red and huge and hungry
where they'll devour me.

Missing, missed

We lived in the same brownstone in Brooklyn, shared clothes, meals, chores. We each had a man who went into Manhattan. We got political together, joined groups protesting the war. We danced to the new relevant rock. We ogled the longhaired men like lustful angels who blossomed suddenly everyplace. Our marriages loosened and we spilled out.

Sometimes we shared lovers. Sometimes you stole men I was flirting with. Finally we made love and you fled into something that felt less dangerous but wasn't.

After a few years of silence, we began to write from opposite coasts and you came to visit me. A whirlwind of fragments of undealt with past spun around you till the air was heavy with noise and flying objects.

Every six months you found true love. You met a charismatic Mexican politico and followed him to Paris. And disappeared. No address, no internet presence, no Facebook, all connections broken. No one knew what had happened to you, dead or alive.

> Darkness swirls
> a hole still darker
> no one there

Death's charming face

I greet dragonflies zipping
into the garden like fighter planes
glinting red, turquoise, transparent
as they attack their prey.

Why are predators often gorgeous?
The tiger prowling like striped silk
rippling: the leopard, ocelot,
the polar most beautiful of bears.

Even sharks have their streamlined
aesthetic. Moon snails that drill
clams to death have shells
beachgoers seek to collect.

Pythons are patterned like Oriental
rugs. Hawks we find majestic
as they soar tiny and crying
mate to mate, then dive talons

outstretched to mangle their prey.
How often women have dashed
themselves senseless on killers
in anthems and arias of blood.

The frost moon

The frost moon like a stone wheel
rolls up the sky. The grass is tipped,
the green life pressed out of weeds
and flowers alike.

A morning powdered with white
and then as the sun inches up
into the trees, glitter. Sequins
rhinestones, broken glass.

Finally it dissolves into the air
leaving stalks that look scorched,
a rim of ice in the shadows,
dry wigs of petals.

The birds mob the feeders.
No moths, no flies, no hoppers
just an occasional bright or drab
leaf eddying down.

Sun still warms the skin or fur
through glass, but the outside
air bites the nose and ears,
the wind whispers hunger.

At night we feel the earth
like a fast freight train hurtling
into the darkness that closes
around us like a tunnel.

December arrives like an unpaid bill

The moon is a fishhook of bone.
Shoals of grey clouds dart past it.
Occasionally one seems to catch
and hang. Tomorrow it will be bigger

sticking like a slice of cantaloupe
out of the sea. Every day less sun
as it crawls out of the seabed later
and sinks into the hill of pines

long before supper. The birds turn
avid at the feeders. The flocks
of wild turkeys grow, the tom
collecting his harem if he pleases

them, or they'll drift to another.
The tail of the red fox is bushy
and he hunts earlier. Every tree
even the stubborn oaks that

clutched tight to their ragged
brown leaves are stripped,
turned to wooden bouquets.
Time to haul wood for the fire.

Time to heap more protection
on the hardy parsnips and pluck

the last nubs of Brussels sprouts
and pull the kale leaves like tough

green lace and dig the final leeks.
Batten down, hill up, stow. We're
heading out into the stormy seas
of winter, no safe harbor in sight.

III

The poor are no longer with us

The suicide of dolphins

No one, not even the scientists who study
you, knows why you beach yourselves
whole family groups, communities
on our beige sand to gasp and die

unless the volunteers, called phone
to phone quickly in a spiderweb
of summoning, can keep you wet
and push you into deep water again

like shoving a huge wet sofa. Some
think it's disease or following your
leader into danger or chasing fish
into water too shallow so you run

aground. An old fisherman said to
me, they remember how they used
to live on the land, they remember.
We know nothing but still we grieve.

Is your act any more opaque than a friend
who drinks himself into a fiery crash?
Another who burnt his brain to a crisp
on crack; the woman who could not

walk out on her husband even after the fifth
trip to the emergency ward, leaving only

feet first when he shot her? Or my friend's
daughter who hanged herself at fifteen

because of names she was called,
because of words on a computer
screen, because of a boy. We cannot
stop each other but still we grieve.

The poor are no longer with us

No one's poor any longer. Listen
to politicians. They mourn the middle
class which is shrinking as we watch
in the mirror. The poor have been

discarded already into the oblivion
pail of not to be spoken words.
They are as lepers were treated once,
to be shipped off to fortified islands

of the mind to rot quietly. If
poverty is a disease, quarantine
its victims. If it's a social problem
imprison them behind high walls.

Maybe it's genetic: how often they
catch easily preventable diseases.
Feed them fast garbage and they'll
die before their care can cost you,

of heart attacks, stroke. Provide
cheap guns and they'll kill each
other well out of your sight.
Ghettos are such dangerous places.

Give them schools that teach
them how stupid they are. But

always pretend they don't exist
because they don't buy enough,

spend enough, give you bribes
or contributions. No ads target
their feeble credit. They are not
real people like corporations.

Don't send dead flowers

There is your mother, your son, your friend
with their insides sucked out, organs
in the sewage, that primped body
filled with carcinogenic chemicals
painted, pinned, presented for your
enjoyment like plastic fruit in a bowl.

Everybody is supposed to coo,
simper, doesn't she look as if
she's sleeping. But she's stone dead
and half of her gone missing now.
An organ oozes lugubrious sound.
Dead flowers surround the corpse.

I want to go into the earth quickly,
quietly and give my minerals back.
I want to become the living soil,
home of beetles and yes, worms.
Let my flesh feed and my bones
fertilize. Gone not to dust but dirt,

the mother of us all. Coffins
like limousines, like Mercedes

expensive and shiny for the left-
overs of a person, pretending
death is a nap and people are
permanent marble monuments.

My flesh tears easily, bruises,
will rot and stink and finally end
sweet as compost, giving itself
to trees, to grass, to wildflowers
and bees and mice, to whatever
wants to grow from my spent life.

A hundred years since the Triangle Fire

On March 25, 1911, a fire spread through the seventh, eighth and ninth floors of the Triangle Shirtwaist Factory in New York City's Greenwich Village. The mostly immigrant workers, young Italian, Jewish, and German women who sewed shirtwaists, or women's blouses, were trapped behind locked doors. The death toll was 146, and many women, their clothing and hair burning, threw themselves from the windows to their deaths on the pavement far below, while spectators watched and could not help. Shortly thereafter, twenty thousand women struck for improved working conditions and wages. The factory building is now part of New York University. The Triangle Shirtwaist Factory Fire remains the fourth largest industrial disaster in U.S. history.

Bodies falling through the air
when all exits from the fire are closed
to them and flames lick their skin:
we have seen that.
In our time and theirs.
Labor was cheap then;
too often cheap now, sweat
shops, whether crammed into
Brooklyn lofts or shipped
overseas. Women are cheap and
children are cheaper. Doors
locked against their escape.

Growing up in center city
Detroit when the factories
hummed like huge hives
at night and the sky was pink
from steel mills on the river
I learned early how replaceable
we all were to those with
power to replace us.
I see your charred clothes
glued to flesh as you hurtle
toward pavement, my sisters,
hard worked women with
blistered hands, forced to labor
six days, whose rest came
only in histories that can never
rectify what greed ignited.

Ethics for Republicans

An embryo is precious;
a woman is a vessel.

A fertilized egg is a person;
a woman is indentured to it.

An embryo is sacred until birth.
After that, he/she is on their own.

Abortion is murder. Rape,
incest are means to an end:

that precious fertilized egg
housed in an expendable body.

Let us make babies and babies
and babies; children are something

else, probably future criminals,
probably welfare cheats whose

education hikes taxes. You
can freely dispose of them.

Another obituary

We were filled with the strong wine
of mutual struggle, one joined loud
and sonorous voice. We carried
each other along revolting, chanting,
cursing, crafting, making all new.

First Muriel, then Audre and Flo,
now Adrienne. I feel like a lone
pine remnant of virgin forest
when my peers have met the ax
and I weep ashes.

Yes, young voices are stirring now,
the wind is rising, the sea boils
again, yet I feel age sucking
the marrow from my bones,
the loneliness of memory.

Their voices murmur in my inner
ear but never will I hear them
speak new words and no matter
how I cherish what they gave us
I want more, I still want more.

What it means

Unemployed: soon invisible,
after a while, unemployable,
unwanted, with your future
eroding along with confidence,
sense of self, the family
cracking along old fault lines.
And what do you *do?* Age.

Out of work: out of security,
out of value, out of the routine
that organizes the days, out
of health insurance, out of
the house when the mortgage
can't be paid, out on the street,
out of society, out of luck.

Your job was shipped
overseas. Your job and two
others are being done now
by one frantic worker.
A robot replaced you.
Your company was bought
and demolished.

•

Somebody elected you
superfluous, a discard.
Somebody made money;
somebody bought a yacht
with your old salary. Some-
body has written you off,
Somebody is killing you.

At night when you can no
longer sleep, don't blame your-
self. What could you have
done? Nothing. Choices were
made to fatten dividends,
bloat bonuses, pay for a new
trophy wife and private plane.

You did nothing wrong
except your birth. Wrong
parents. Wrong place. Wrong
race. Wrong sex. If only
you'd had the sense to be
born to the one percent
life would be truffles today.

How have the mighty . . .

What we have done to you
for our convenience. In cave
paintings you stand, huge, looming
over hunters with your sharp
deadly horns and prancing hooves.
You could reach seven feet tall
at your massive shoulders.

Called Aurochs, now just cows.
We have tamed the wildness out,
shrunk you to an amenable size.
You were bigger than bison,
fierce, worshipped for your strength
companions of the moon goddess.
In the Greek islands, dove cotes

sacred to her are marked with
your horns. Hathor the cow
goddess gave fertility and joy.
I meet your limpid gaze as you
chew your cud under a scrub oak
then rise lowing to be milked:
turned from monarch to food.

We know

The crickets are loud at night
a chorus of teakettles demanding
sex. The tomato plants begin
to brown from the bottom up.

South of here a hurricane comes
ashore with murder in its hollow
heart, winds little can stand
against, a surge of tide roiling

over seawalls. The lords of oil
know they will survive however
the soil cracks with drought
and cattle and mustangs die

of thirst. No matter how tornadoes
level towns, strewing the precious
of lives across rubble. Hurricanes
move in posses across the weather

map. We who garden feel climate
change in our dirty hands, see
strange new bugs and stampeding
weeds, piles of eggplants and no

peas, fewer butterflies, more horse-
flies. We face the ocean that is way

too warm this time of year and wait
and worry, but we do not pray

to the lords of oil who control
the climate but to whatever god
we offer our hope like the fruits
Cain brought that were rejected.

The passion of a fan

What part of a person is tied up
in the sports team they watch
on TV? I remember the day after
the Patriots lost the Super Bowl
to the Giants, the streets of Wellfleet
were dim with the fog of depression.

Defeat wafted through houses, offices,
stores. It was yellow-grey and tasted
of salt and pollution. In Byzantium
supporters of green or blue chariot
racing teams killed each other
till the streets ran crimson.

We not only root for our teams
but see wars as giant hockey
games. Our team's basketball
forward is dearer than a neighbor
or cousin or co-worker. He
is our darling, our avatar.

Somehow we seek to become him.
We wear his number. We
imagine he would love us

back. But we don't exist.
We're just noise in the stadium,
so many numbered ticket holders,

sad faces, autograph seekers
a maw into which that player's
talent is leeched until glory
days are over and he retires
to fail at a restaurant and die
at fifty-eight of an enlarged heart.

In pieces

Governments, TV newsmen count soldiers
dead, wounded—mostly the dead, never
the brain dead or the damaged in what
passes for life, the suicides, the trained
killers who can't stop loading their anger.

But mostly that's not who dies from
a drone attacking a suspicious crowd
that is really a market. Just caught
in crossfire. The wrong place [their
little house] wrong time [family meal].

A school is poisoned, a wedding
party is strafed, a hospital is blown
up. Babies are collateral damage.
A pregnant woman may be hiding
a bomb in her maternity clothes.

The dogs, the cats, the birds tame
and wild, the cattle, goats, lizards,
hares, foxes, all the creatures who
live in what has become a battlefield
and have no way to safety: they die.

Trees perish; whole forests, whole
ecosystems are bombed out of
existence. Creeks poisoned. Soil

honeycombed with mines. Farms
vanished. Ways of living destroyed.

After armies have gone back home
where taxes still pay for that war,
how many decades will pass until
the land is green and fertile again,
people do not scream in their sleep

if they dare to sleep, children play
in fields without losing a leg or head,
birds sing celebrating their nests,
neighbors forgive desperate choices
and a thing ripped is finally knit whole.

Ghosts

How often we navigate by what is no
longer there. Turn right where the post
office used to be. She lives in a condo
above where the bakery blew sweet
yeasty smells into the street. A nail
salon now.

Kelsey Hayes had a factory there
on Livernois where our neighbors
worked. A foundry spat out metal
where the strip club spits neon
now and loud skanky music
into the night.

Rows of little cheap houses replaced
by a few McMansions. Where did
all those people go? The workers
in factories, in tool and die shops,
the shoemakers and tailors, mom
and pop eateries?

You can be plunked down in Anywhere
U.S.A. and see the same row of stores
Target, Walmart, Gap, Toys-R-Us.
Exit the superhighway: McDonald's,

Taco Bell, Burger King, Hardees,
you haven't moved.

That's where the school was: see,
it's condos now. That's the church
the parish closed to pay for priests'
sex. China got the shoe factory.
Urban renewal turned the old neighbor-
hood to dust.

Some things we make better and some
are destroyed by greed and bad
politics. We live in the wake
of decisions we didn't share in,
survivors of a vast lethal typhoon
of power.

One of the expendables

Cape Cod is wed to the mainland
by two bridges, on mild week
ends and all summer fed
by miles of backed up cars.

Right across Massachusetts
Bay, one of the worst nuclear
power plants, clone of Fukushima
leaks into the bay. On its roof

three thousand spent rods.
Vulnerable to hurricane, flooding,
attack from the air or land,
it squats menacing us.

We who live here all year, our
hundred thousands of summer
visitors, we have been deemed
expendable since we cannot

by any means be evacuated.
"Shelter in place" means breathe
in, absorb through your skin,
drink, swallow, eat radiation.

Your home will be uninhabitable
should you happen to survive

at least a while before cancer
dissolves your organs. The land

the pure water we cherish
will be tainted for decades. Fish,
birds, your dog and cats, raccoons,
squirrels, coywolves expendable

too. We count for nothing
compared to profits for a utility
housed in New Orleans where
you'd imagine they know floods.

We're the throwaway people,
not important like corporations.
Chop off the crooked arm
of Cape Cod and let us bleed.

Let's meet in a restaurant

Is food the enemy?
Giving a dinner party has become
an ordeal. I lie awake the night
before figuring how to produce

a feast that is vegan, gluten free,
macrobiotic, avoiding all acidic
fruit and tomatoes, wine, all nuts,
low carb and still edible.

Are beetles okay for vegans?
Probably not. Forget chocolate
ants or fried grasshoppers.
Now my brains are cooked.

Finally seven o'clock arrives
and I produce the perfect meal.
At each plate for supper, a bowl
of cleanly washed pebbles. Enjoy!

My time in better dresses

I remember job hunting in my shoddy
and nervous working class youth,
how I had to wear nylons and white
gloves that were dirty in half an hour
for jobs that barely paid for shoes.

Don't put down Jew, my mother
warned, *just say Protestant, it
doesn't commit you to anything.*
Ads could still say "white" and
in my childhood, we weren't.

I worked in better dresses in Sam's
cut-rate department store, $3.98
and up. I wasn't trusted to sell.
I put boxes together, wrapped,
cleaned out dressing rooms.

My girlfriend and I bought a navy
taffeta dress with cutout top, wore it
one or the other to parties, till it failed
my sophistication test. The older
"girls" in sales, divorced, sleek,

impressed me, but the man in charge
I hated, the way his eyes stroked,
stripped, discarded. How he docked
our pay for lateness. How he sucked
on his power like a piece of candy.

Come fly without me

A ship in a bottle looks stately
if arcane and somewhat archaic.
But two hundred people crammed
into a flying bottle breathing
filthy air is disgusting.

Come stuff your carry-on
into a mail slot so you can be
parked on the tarmac for eight
hours while the toilet overflow
runs down the aisle. Hungry?

Buy 10 stale potato chips
for six dollars. Come ride
with your knees digging hard
into your chin. When the guy
in front leans back, your tray

will slam your stomach. Fly
the germy skies inhaling TB.
The pilots have been awake
for seventeen hours and can't
see the controls.

The plane was last serviced
by drunk mechanics who used
to fix pinball machines. Enjoy
your delayed overbooked flight
as the airlines enjoy your money.

These bills are long unpaid

To predict disaster, to invoke treachery
and malice, to spin tales of rotten
luck to make it not happen:
that doesn't work.

The wind is still rising with hail
in its teeth. The waves are piling up
then spilling way, way back baring
bottom you've never seen.

There's ashes in the wind, darling,
a taste of ashes in our food
ashes on our lips in bed
eyes blinded with ash.

There's a mortgage on my spine
I cannot pay. Somebody has
bought my teeth and wants them
out tomorrow for dice.

There are real monsters under
the bed, hungry for blood. They own
the land this house stands on
to stripmine for coal.

Santa isn't coming. The bounty
hunter is. There's a lien on your

ass and the bank is itchy to fore
close your future.

If you're going to stand, get up.
If you're going to fight, get moving.
Nothing comes to those who wait
but hunger's claws

digging into the soft belly. If you
value your blood, fight to keep
it in your veins. You have nothing
to lose but your life

and it was sold to them decades
ago by your parents' parents.
Their greed is endless. Your
patience shouldn't be.

Hope is a long, slow thing

"I became a feminist but I didn't
get it all so I have committed to
the Church of Perpetual Subservience."

"I protested, demonstrated but still
the war went on, so I have realized
politics is useless and have joined

The Junior League instead. We have
marvelous luncheons." "I made phone
calls for my candidate but little

happened so I'll never vote again."
But progress is never individual.
A wave crashes on our shore, traveling

all the way from Africa, storming,
eroding the cliff, grinding it down
but the same water is not what moved.

We are droplets in a wave. Maybe
I cannot with my efforts displace
a rock but the energy of a movement

can force it from the way. Look back:

My great-grandmother was killed
in a pogrom. My grandmother gave

birth to eleven children in a tenement
eating potatoes only sometimes. My
mother had to leave school in tenth grade

to work as a chambermaid that salesmen
chased around dirty beds. Nothing
changed by itself but *was* changed by work.

History records no progress people
did not sweat and dare to push. A long
"we" is the power that moves the rock.

IV

Working at it

The late year

I like Rosh Hashanah late,
when the leaves are half burnt
umber and scarlet, when sunset
marks the horizon with slow fire
and the black silhouettes
of migrating birds perch
on the wires davening.

I like Rosh Hashanah late
when all living are counting
their days toward death
or sleep or the putting by
of what will sustain them—
when the cold whose tendrils
translucent as a jellyfish

and with a hidden sting
just brush our faces
at twilight. The threat
of frost, a premonition,

a warning, a whisper
whose words we cannot
yet decipher, but will.

I repent better in the waning
season when the blood
runs swiftly and all creatures
look keenly about them
for quickening danger.
Then I study the rock face
of my life, its granite pitted

and pocked and pickaxed,
eroded, discolored by sun
and wind and rain—
my rock emerging
from the veil of greenery
to be mapped, to be
examined, to be judged.

Erev New Years

This is my real new year's eve,
not that mishmash of desperate
parties with somebody puking
on your shoes or passing out,

that night when amateur drunks
crash into telephone poles
or other drivers. Here I make
my real resolutions as I toss

breadcrumbs into the Herring
River as it pours into Wellfleet
Bay. I try, but some sins,
some failures I toss year after

year and still they lurk in me.
Every Rosh Hashanah I swear
to be less impatient, then fail,
but next year, fresh and sweet

marked with honey and apples,
surely I will correct myself.
My year opens its bronze doors
and I pass through into whatever

the Book holds and whatever
I make or unmake or pass by.
I walk into this new beginning
of a self still under construction.

Head of the year

Head of the year and time to use
our heads: to think deeply without
subterfuge, without excuses—flaking
them off the worn bones of last
year's resolutions.

How pitiful they look now, remnants
of kavanah more like rags than
the skeletal foundation on which
we planned to build our forceful
and gracious new year.

Every Rosh Hashanah I make
some of the same resolves. Where
does that energy leak off to? Are
they just perfunctory gestures
at this new year?

Which resolves did I start carrying
out fresh and eager and then let
slide? Which were real only on
paper, Potemkin villages of the mind,
never made new—

nice facades I didn't truly mean to
inhabit. Tomorrow as I do tashlich
let me make no paper promises
but carry these resolves into action
in this still sweet new year.

May the new year continue our joy

Apples and honey for the new year
but you are my year round sweet
apple. The apple of my eye, apple
of temptation and delight. My honey:

our lives together are full of work,
harvest from dirt and sweat, bounty
of work from the brain and the heart,
we're each other's wages and prize:

the seeds in every apple, the flower
and the pollen and the nectar
and the final ultimate honey
our bodies make and surrender.

I was never truly happy before you.
I was never truly whole before you.

Late that afternoon they come

At Yizkor my dead swim around me
schools of them flashing, then
slowly as one by one I honor them.

Mother, brother, bobbah, aunts,
uncles, cousins, I am here to say
one by one silently their names.

Friends of all the times of my life,
those who left young, those whom
death took after illness ravaged them;

those whose names shine for all,
those who lived hidden by poverty,
those whom you might call ordinary

but not to those who loved them.
My cats come too, even if you
believe they lack souls. All those

I've loved and cherished circle
in the fading light of Yizkor and I
pray, blessed be their memories.

As long as I live let me pause to
remember, let me pay them a prayer
placed like a stone on their graves.

N'eilah

The hinge of the year
the great gates opening
and then slowly slowly
closing on us.

I always imagine those gates
hanging over the ocean
fiery over the stone grey
waters of evening.

We cast what we must
change about ourselves
onto the waters flowing
to the sea. The sins,

errors, bad habits, whatever
you call them, dissolve.
When I was little I cried
out I! I! I! I want I want.

Older, I feel less important,
a worker bee in the hive
of history, miles of hard
labor to make my sweetness.

The gates are closing
The light is failing

I kneel before what I love
imploring that it may live.

So much breaks, wears
down, fails in us. We must
forgive our failed promises—
their broken glass in our hands.

The wall of cold descends

Near the end of our annual solstice party
as guests were rummaging through the pile
for their coats and hugging many goodbyes
the very first snow of the year began
to eddy down in big flat flakes.

It was cold enough to stick, with the grass
poking through and then buried.
Now the ground gives it back
under the low ruddy sun that sits
on the boughs of the pine like a fox

if red foxes could climb. The cats
crowd the windows for its touch.
The Wolf Moon seemed bigger than
the sun, almost brighter as last night
it turned the snow ghostly.

Now it too wanes. The nub end
of the year when all northern
cultures celebrate fire and light.
Tonight we'll take the first two candles
to kindle one from the other.

When we go out after dark, our
eyes seek lights that bore holes

in the thick black like the pelt
of a huge hairy monster, a grizzly
who devours the warm-blooded.

We are kin with the birds who huddle
in evergreens, who crowd feeders,
kin with the foxes and their prey, kin
with all who shiver this night, home-
less or housed, clutching or alone

under the vast high dome of night.

How she learned

A friend was an only child, she thought,
until sorting through her mother's things
after the frail old woman died—who
had borne Anna late in life, a miracle,
a blessing, she was always told—

Anna found a greying photograph.
Her aunt who escaped Poland
in '37 had saved and given it
to her younger sister who barely
survived Nordhausen working inside

the mountain, skinny almost-ghost.
Anna recognized her mother, decades
younger, but against her side was
pressed a girl not Anna. Scrawled
on the back, *Feygelah und Perl.*

Who was Feygelah? Her aunt bore
only sons. This girl was four or five
with long light braids, her legs
locked together in a shy fit. Who?
There were letters back and forth,

Boston to Krakow. She sat reading
them, puzzling out the handwriting,

the Yiddish. She had a dictionary
but even then, it took her late into
the evening. Anna had a sister.

A sister vanished into smoke.
A sister torn from her mother,
murdered, burnt. Anna sat numb.
She was the replacement for
a girl whose name her mother

could not speak. The weight
of history pressed on Anna's chest
that night and finally she wept—
mourning the sister never known
and her mother's decades of silence.

Working at it

So much in Tanakh is a mixed
bag, a tangled message. Eliyahu
and Elisha come to the Jordan;
the elder prophet strikes the water
and parts it for them. He makes

a safe dry road through what
would drown them. We all try
to do that for those we cherish.
Elisha resists show—fiery
horses and chariot—and witnesses

the whirlwind and is rewarded
with Eliyahu's spiritual power.
He too can part the waters.
We hope for the gifts our mentors
have tried to teach us, to carry on.

When he travels, boys mock
his bald head and he sends bears
to savage forty-two children.
What can I learn from this? To take
myself seriously into violence?

We pick and choose what to
cherish of those tales, our minds
picking at them for spiritual sense
so we can part the dangerous waters
of our time to cross our Jordans.

The order of the seder

The songs we join in
are beeswax candles
burning with no smoke
a clean fire licking at the evening

our voices small flames quivering.
The songs string us like beads
on the hour. The ritual is
its own melody that leads us

where we have gone before
and hope to go again, the comfort
of year after year. Order:
we must touch each base

of the haggadah as we pass,
blessing, handwashing,
dipping this and that. Voices
half harmonize on the brukhahs.

Dear faces like a multitude
of moons hang over the table
and the truest brief blessing:
affection and peace that we make.

The two cities

L'shanah haba'ah b'Yerushalayim
we say every Pesach, concluding
the haggadah. Some say it piously,
some with pride, some almost
embarrassed, some with mixed

feelings, some balk at the words.
In the murderous times that came
down so often in the Diaspora,
it was said with fervent hope
that some where, some time

we could, would belong, be
free. But Jerusalem, the golden,
the city on the hill, is two
cities, one blood-soaked, fought
over for millennia, again, again.

The other is a city of the mind.
Utopia comes as a walled garden
or as a city, a community of peace
we have never reached, where
justice and equality are daily

as water and still as precious.
May we always travel onward

toward that good place even
if like Moses we never arrive
struggling through dust and blood

to unite the two Jerusalems
in one shining city of peace.

Where silence waits

How hard it is to keep Shabbat,
to stop what crams days, evenings
like a hoarder's house and to thrust
every worry, duty, command,

every list of What Is To Be Done
into a mental closet and bolt
that door. We feel half guilty
not to be multitasking.

Surely this space we eke out
is indulgence. Where's
the end product? How can we
walk into silence like a pond?

The computer, the smart phone,
the fax machine summon us
to attend to shrill voices. How
can we justify being idle?

How can we listen to that voice
that issues only from deep
stillness and silence? How
can we ever afford not to?

I say Kaddish but still mourn

Tonight I light the first skinny candles
of celebration and the single fat
candle of grieving, for this first
night is my mother's yahrzeit too.

I say Kaddish that never mentions
death but in me is a hole that never
quite healed over, that sweet lonely
scar of missing that goes on

year after year singing its husky
lament for a tattered life, for lone-
liness inside an asbestos bungalow
where she cleaned and cleaned

and cleaned what could never
be clean, in the fog of acid
and smoke from the factories.
All that was white yellowed.

All that was right passed away.
All that had been soft hardened
to shards of shattered hopes.
All that was promised her, lied.

Yet in that asbestos almost
prison, she delighted in sweets,

in baking what she wanted to eat.
She gobbled books whole,

she held sway over the neighbor
women reading their palms.
Gossip quieted her pain. Others
suffer too, she said. Amein.

V

That was Cobb Farm

Little diurnal tragedies

Mercy for the dog lying broken
backed in the road while the car
that hit it speeds off.

Mercy for the wren baby pushed
from the nest by the bigger hatchling—
egg the cowbird deposited.

Mercy for the green turtles caught
in the sudden cold of the bay
when the nor'easter blows.

Mercy for the pregnant cat thrown
out to starve, nursing her five kittens
among garbage and broken glass.

Mercy for the geese the golfers
want poisoned because they disturb
the green beside already polluted pools.

Mercy for the birds trying to fly
south on ancient routes, blinded
by our lights, dying on skyscrapers.

All around us are creatures we barely

notice, trying to preserve their only
lives among our machinery,

among our smog and smoke, inside
our radiation, among the houses and
roads built on their once habitats.

The next evolutionary step

In the Herring River, the mummichog
lives along with eels, alewives, green
and bullfrogs, snapping turtles
and muskrats. Of all these
the mummichog is the smallest

but the hardiest. It can withstand
heat and cold. Polluted waters
do not sicken it. It survives most
poisons and is predicted to outlive
us all in nuclear disaster.

It schools with hundreds of kin
who move as one through muddy
waters, feeling their way. On
the full moon it releases its eggs
and on the new moon too making

sure there will always be multitudes
of mummichogs. I, who am far
less sure of my survival, salute
you, for in spite of all we do to
destroy, you'll repopulate earth.

That was Cobb Farm

When I drive around my village
poking through half the buildings
are what they used to be: the upscale
gallery I never enter was the post office.

On busy mornings in summer what
car acrobatics were required to pick
up the mail, the parking ample
enough in the winter, now jammed.

The gas station that's turned into pizza;
the restaurant that failed five
different owners and now stands
vacant, its most recent sign fading

to GNR ATO, a warning perhaps
to future entrepreneurs. The fire
station now sells leather clothing
from May to October. Houses

from which friends were rushed
to the hospital to die or brought
back home to do it in peace.
The field where the white horse

Ajax browsed. Once in a thunder
storm, he climbed onto my porch
and stuck his head in the window.
Stood there awhile and then walked

slowly down the drive and away.
The candle factory became the library.
The farm was cut into development lots.
A hurricane brought down a forest

like skinny dominoes, now a field.
The wrecked boat's bones no longer
protrude at low tide. Millionaires'
summer houses fell over the cliff.

Used to be, used to—my head crammed
with useless memories: an attic in
a house someone buys, wondering
why the owner kept all that old junk.

They meet

Lava from an island volcano
plunges into the sea. Vermilion
and black landscape by day,
at night the white torrents
resemble television reports
of rush hour traffic.

Where water and fire
collide, a column of smoke
and steam gushes upward,
water boiling as the lava
did. Nothing living could
survive this fusion.

How it roars as it meets
the water. This is a tropical
sea, not cold but lava
is boiling rock, magma
melting all it touches
till water snuffs it.

Now it turns back to rock.
Excitement. Smoking.
Irresistible fire consuming
all in its path. Till abruptly
it's doused and returns
to a previous state.

So it goes sometimes
with lovers.

A cigarette left smoldering

Walking through the luminous rain
sliding down her bare arms as if
the city wept, she dreamed instead
of fire, drops of it small as beetles.

I could walk through fire, she
thought, but she was wrong. Her
summer dress went up in a single
torch and she screamed

like something torn. I see her face
still, sometimes when I think I am
falling asleep and then don't,
her mouth a perfect circle.

We die different ways. We beg
to go painlessly as rain falling.

Discovery motion

The kitten from the shelter hasn't
learned her name Xena yet. But how
wonderful that leap: those nonmeows
humans utter mean something.

When I mention her name, Puck
turns his head and looks at her.
He has grasped that noises belong
to beings and objects and actions:

out, chicken, no, come, sit. How
does a creature without language
suddenly put that attachment to-
gether? Human babies preprogrammed

to stare at faces, still take a while.
They babble long before they speak.
Then there's the long learning process
that words are not the thing,

that promises only shape air, that
cries of passion are nonnegotiable,
that we walk through our days
followed by biting swarms of lies.

Sun in January

An icy wind down from Quebec
freezes the homeless teenager
sleeping in a carton under
the rumble of a highway bridge.

Walking in High Toss, I find
the corpse of a dog some
hunter shot. By accident?
In anger? For sport? To

the dog, why would that
matter, the paws outstretched
as if to beg, head chin down
between them, flies swarming.

A friend is back in chemo.
All food tastes like metal,
she says. *I have no appetite.*
It's the third time of poison.

Today the whole world shines
as if someone polished every
single twig. The air is vanilla
ice cream. We are warm together.

So much can go wrong
we are almost afraid to be happy.

Little rabbit's dream song

I will be safe in the grass.
I will be as safe as I was
when my mother cuddled me
in the high grass.

I will have plenty to eat.
I will have not only the wild
grasses and tender fruit
but carrots and cabbage.

No dog will see me, no
coywolf, no prowling cat.
No hawk will spy me
from a dot in the sky.

I will be safe and full.
I will be warm as when
my mother cuddled me
content in the high grass.

Let it be so, let it be
so, let it be so all
the sun and into the dark
when the coywolves howl.

Different voices, one sentence

I love you in one voice is an arrival,
in another a curse. It can be a wall
imprisoning. Or a door opening
to who knows what pain or joy.

When it's spoken sometimes
the listener flinches, wants to
force it back into the mouth
that dropped it like a net.

Sometimes it has been waited
for so long it has lost its juice
wizened now, a winter potato
in the bottom of the sack.

Sometimes we fall into it
willing to take what we can get.

Cotton's wife

She knows she is right at breakfast,
the correct cereal with fatless milk.
Afterward she runs herself gaunt.
I weigh less at forty than at fourteen,
she confides to just about everyone.

In the mirror an aura of sanctity.
Her husband will not love her
if she is not perfect, flat, hard
as a landing strip. His disapproval
frosts their bed and her blood.

He is the voice of the Puritan
father. He channels Cotton Mather
and dreams of burning native villages
full of naked sinners, of hanging
uppity women who mutter charms.

She reads the fine print on every
bottle, in every manual. Her
mattresses still sport their tags.
Life is a marathon that keeps
getting longer. Her nipples bleed.

The Puritan's wife becomes a pillar
of rock, an obelisk pointing toward
the cold grey sky—a monument
commemorating a girl who tried
to grow into a woman but was pruned.

That summer day

The morning of the day you died
the birds were singing backup
to a huge red sun
marching out of the green marsh.

Later as your breath was rasping
that sun now fiery white
beat on the blue gong of the sky
and the birds were silent.

The squash blossoms were opening
to warmth. A bumblebee zizzed
its way through the garden. A striped
caterpillar mounted the dill.

A robin ate it in two gulps. Later
a ruddy fox looked at me from
under the pitch pines, eyeing
the tabby in the window.

Everybody went about their daily
round, chasing and being chased,
flying, trotting, eating, eaten while
you were slowly swallowed

and we wept.

Insomniac prayer at 2 a.m.

Sleep winds around me like a coy
snake, touching, squeezing, feinting
withdrawing. Tedious foreplay
never arriving at the act itself.

Or the absence of act: that place
I can let go of the day and allow
problems to fall like a tray of dishes
breaking, except that in the morning

every problem is seamlessly intact.
I'm a tightrope walker who longs
to let go, to dive into that sweet fog
below. Rise up, fog, and engulf me,

melt me into you. Let me cease
all the brain and body's muttering,
the discontents of organ and joint.
Let me be Nobody—no body, no

mind nattering, no ambitions,
losses, bills, projects, obligations:
let nothing fill me like a deserted hall
where words no longer resonate.

I want to be emptied out, a purse
dumped on the table. Sleep, you
are the only room I long to enter
that moon of white silence.

The body in the hot tub

The day was planned, birthday
of two friends, Indian food.
They had secured the ingredients
mail order two weeks before.

The day was preordered, time
to make the mango chutney, time
to wash the rice, to pound spices
in the mortar, soak chickpeas.

The police pounded on the door
at six a.m., sent the couple
and their dog into exile from
a crime scene: a nude woman

facedown in their tenant's
hot tub. No, they had heard
nothing. The dog had not barked,
he slept with them. A quiet night.

Our ordered days can crack open
like an egg dropped on the floor,
its contents leaking out
in a sticky yellow mess.

A woman they had never met
dying on their land, who knew

how or why, the tub itself
now a grisly souvenir,

the police busy with questions
they couldn't begin to answer—
and the one we all ask, why
me? why us? why today?

VI

Looking back in utter confusion

Looking back in utter confusion

Sometimes I think I am a fiction
and only memories strung together
hold my life to some coherence.

If all my lovers stood in a line
what commonality would I see
except luck good and bad,

except need and accident,
desperation like a bad cough
recurring to convulse my body.

If all the clothes I wore were strung
on a blocklong clothesline, I'd see
not decoration but roles, all

in a row, selves slipped into, now
too tight, too loose, too short.
Discarded for a new foray.

But if my cats were lined up
I'd know exactly how I loved each
their games, their habits, how

they lived with me and died

leaving me. If all the edicts
I put forth, manifestos, diatribes,

all those didactic moments came
swarming, I'd duck and run. I
was so sure. Then not. Then not

at all. Yet I go stumbling on
bearing my nametag still wonder-
ing how I came to get here.

Why did the palace of excess have cockroaches?

Why did I get drunk so often in college? Because I was a writer and I had read many biographies of writers and they drank. If I was a writer and writers drank to excess, then I must drink till I passed out, even though that scared me. Why did I try mescaline, drop acid, eat as much hash as I could get in the late '60s and early '70s? Because all my heroes said that enlightenment came in pill form, through dope. I wanted to be wise. I wasn't. I did not find much to guide me in my vivid hallucinations although I did speak with the dead. They had little to say except to resent their dying. I told them how I missed them but they didn't listen. Blake said that the road to wisdom leads through the palace of excess, but all I got was in bed with a couple of louts and really bad nightmares that hung on like red fog after I woke.

> Cold water dripping
> on granite with patience makes
> a deep enough hole.

In the Peloponnesus one April afternoon

Wild red poppies blanketed the hills.
As I perched on a sun warmed rock
I felt breath on my neck. A half-grown
goat looked into my eyes with her
knowing yellow gaze, nibbled my collar.

I had climbed halfway up a mountain
and the sun stuck to my black hair
a too heavy helmet. In the distance,
small bells jangled. The cry of a circling
hawk sliced the air like a scimitar.

Bits of marble were jumbled around me,
some unknown unnamed ruin that people
once had cared enough to build, hauling
pale blocks up a steeply angled slope.
Temple, I wondered, to what kind of god?

A god of goats, the yellow eyes suggested.
She bleated for emphasis. A dancing creature
horned and horny, celebrated with food
and orgy, worshippers leaping and turning,
feet pounding the ground, the feet that started

poetry going forward one beat at a time.
I had no wine, so I poured a little sip
from my canteen on the ground and bent
my head in homage to what had been
sacred and in my mind, still was.

The end not yet in sight

It was a taut time, bitter and bitten.
I lived part of the time with a man
I had married but who had pried
open the marriage years before
so he could chase the young
and easy girls sprouting around us.

I thought of you as I cooked, burning
liver. I thought of you as I bathed
my otherwise untouched body
gleaming underwater as if I swam
in tears. I thought of you and I
felt a hot acid pain in my gut.

Longing ripped through me
making new roads of absence.
My desire was a strange creature
that lived in my chest and ate
at me with its ferocious teeth.
I thought we could never

really be a couple, because
I was trapped in his plots
and needs and secret angers

like snakes under the floorboards.
I was alone in a crowded house
wallpapered with rancid blame.

I could see no doors, only
windows in which you wandered
just in the range of my sight.
In the cage of my gone-bad
marriage I turned my gerbil
wheel of despair ever faster.

Loving clandestinely

I carried my love for you hidden
like cash stuffed into a bra.
Cooking, cleaning, sitting with
friends, I was secretly absent,
my inner attention cocooned
around your face.

I called myself idiot. Fan-
tasy was a drug; I was its
addict, rushing to consume
it every moment. I dreamed
the impossible escape
to your bed.

It was like a song I couldn't
keep from taking over
my brain where it repeated
repeated repeated. Stupefied
with desire, nothing I did
was quite real.

Only those moments we stole
before planes, in the woods,
while he went off with girl
friends or buddies, that
was my true and only life
until it was.

The visible and the in-

Some people move through your life
like the perfume of peonies, heavy
and sensual and lingering.

Some people move through your life
like the sweet musky scent of cosmos
so delicate if you sniff twice, it's gone.

Some people occupy your life
like moving men who cart off
couches, pianos and break dishes.

Some people touch you so lightly you
are not sure it happened. Others leave
you flat with footprints on your chest.

Some are like those fall warblers
you can't tell from each other even
though you search Petersen's.

Some come down hard on you like
a striking falcon and the scars remain
and you are forever wary of the sky.

We all are waiting rooms at bus

stations where hundreds have passed
through unnoticed and others

have almost burned us down
and others have left us clean and new
and others have just moved in.

What's left

What marks does a marriage leave
when one of them has gone
into another entanglement?

A bottle of wine chosen, forgotten.
A old cat dying slowly of kidney
failure. Some books no longer

valued, music of another decade
they used to dance to, back
when dancing was together.

A green wool sweater abandoned
in the corner of a closet. Railroad
tie steps they buried in the hillside.

Trees they planted now taller
than the house. A mask, a wooden
necklace from foreign travels.

Pain drying up like a pond dying
from the edges but still deep
enough in the center to drown.

Corner of Putnam and Pearl

We rented an apartment on Putnam
and Pearl at a stop sign where music
blared from cars all night boasting
their taste before they gunned away.

The top floor under the flat tar roof
was sodden with heat. Next door
on the steps of the halfway house
men drank from paper bags.

Always some dog was barking
like a saw cutting into rough wood.
Sirens blasted tunnels in thick
air and below, someone cursed.

Oddly, we were happy there,
our love still moist and sticky
a mousse that had not quite jelled
but sweet with ripe strawberries.

You came home at two reeking
of smoke and garlic, high from
restaurant drugs and afterwork
drinks with kitchen crews.

I banged away on my Olympia
typewriter, trying to pay off

debts from my bloody divorce.
We were growing into each

other, tentative roots like fragile
tentacles exploring the other's
body and brain. By the time we
moved, we'd knotted to a couple.

Bang, crash over

Breakage. Yes, splinters, the shards
pierce my brain. In each friendship,
a new self grows different from any
other of the selves we make and unmake.
In every love however small as marbles
children roll in their palms and stare into,
we become. In the big ones, our faces
change and never quite resume.

So a piece tears off after the final
quarrel, after the argument that burned
the night to cinders and a wind of grey
ashes, after the wind has dispersed
even the last smear of ash and nothing
nothing at all stays but a friendship
whose dead weight hangs from your
neck like the sailor's albatross, quite

murdered but still of sufficient weight
to bend your back. Your neck hurts.
Words clot in your throat like blood.
A lot of you hurts. Pain grabs attention
but is boring as it spikes and drones
on and on. *Shut up* you scream at it
at three a.m. But in the end months
years pass and you forget. Almost.

Sins of omission

Suppose hell were a room
where the lovers you broke
up with, the spouses you left,
the friends you discarded

all were waiting to question
you, with no time limit ever
but the explanations could last
halfway into eternity. Who

wouldn't sooner leap into
a fire? There is no excuse
for the end of love or for
the fact that it never started

its engine into that lovely
roar but just coughed again
and again until you gave up
and got out and went off.

Some friendships are just not
sturdy enough to bear the daily
wear and weight. How to say,
but simply you bored me.

Then all the people you did
not help, the ones you hung

up on, letters unanswered,
loans denied, calls not returned

that endless line will be snaking
through the horizon, waiting
to demand what you would
not give, life's unpaid bills.

Even if we try not to let go

Our minds cannot hold the dead.
They seep away. Their voices,
gone to silence no matter how
hard I try to cup them in my ear.

Their faces come apart, cubist
explosions of dark eyes, blue,
grey green, her nose, his flyaway
hair, the crumpled skin of hands.

Did she really say that? Or was
it April instead of October? What
year did measles hit? The color
of her red dress with fishscale sequins.

Did the glass break when he slammed
the door? He told that joke forty
times at least. Then suddenly he
laughs in my hair and I know him.

How we come apart in death,
not only our bodies decomposing
but our lives, stuck in random
pieces in the brains of others

who loved or hated us, who carry
us in memory or in their genes, who
slowly must let us drift like autumn
leaves down to the final ground.

Afterward

We lie inert half open and spent
like flowers just past peak, loosened
but gloriously scented. When
a couple loves intensely, we
are even closer after sex than
during. More content. We still
touch but lightly in a kind of lull
that is totally complete.

We never ask, how was that
for you, because we know.
Practice makes whatever
of perfection we can have.
No longer joined at genitals
but in a larger longer joining
two meandering hard flowing
rivers melding into one.

We lie at peace on the sunporch
the woods all around us, wrens
tittering, a dragonfly just over
us on the translucent roof,
two cats snoozing one on each
red cushion and Xena watching
those wrens through the screen.
Everybody is safe. Today. Now.

The wonder of it

The wonder of it, building a home
in one another after so many false
starts, collapses, fires set
intentionally or by default,
paper houses the cold winds
blew into shreds.

Our foundation was tentative
enough, part-time. We began
with a rickety lean-to propped
against the walls of previous
matings. Then brick of trust
by brick we laid

this structure in which we
dwell, decade upon decade,
adding a room here, a bay
window to let the sun come
in, a new roof to keep out
the wind and snow.

Repairing is work that never
lets up, always some leak or stained
wall, loose floorboard, burnt
out plug. But we'll never leave
this house except feet first
on a final stretcher.

Marinade for an elderly rabbit

NOTE ON A RECIPE IN A COOKBOOK

I could use some time in a marinade
myself. Perhaps Madeira on winter
evenings. A nice refreshing Chablis.

Champagne would be ritzy but ticklish.
A nice dry martini bath on hot days
would soften me up nicely.

Some days I feel leathery
as a snapping turtle. Some days
I am dry as burnt pie dough.

Some days the winds of trouble
have left me scorched and crumbly.
Sometimes I'm just a bald tire.

Yes, prepare me a marinade, dear.
Soak me in it overnight. Tomorrow
you'll find me far easier to digest.

Contemplating my breasts

Strange, these soft lumps on my front.
Like men with their pricks, women
whose breasts are large tend to be
somewhat obsessed with you.

We are always having to watch out
for you, pick out bras with the care
men spend selecting a new car.
Can't lie on my stomach for long.

Watch you don't get bumped too
hard. Notice blouses won't button
when otherwise they fit just fine.
Men stare at them when addressing

me as if my nipples were talking.
Some of us are selfconscious,
wearing muumuus and sweat
shirts or layer over layer. Others

seek clothes that show you off.
My identity contains a streak
of you. But sometimes I feel
as if I walk around behind you

like a person behind a parade
float, just tagging along.

Words hard as stones

All the words I never spoke in time
in the flashing moments when they
could have, might have but didn't—
they follow me like vultures circling

so that I know something rotten
lies in the field. The apologies
never delivered age in the dead
letter office of the brain, yellowing.

But the promises' broken bits
have worked their way into
the mattress and poke my sleep,
words I should never have said.

Gossip, curses, whispers behind
closed doors, in bed; words
hurled in argument, justification,
the stinging gnats of lies:

sticky words, overpoweringly
fragrant like lilies in a closed room,
rancid, spiky. Such are words made
flesh, made bread, made dagger.

Absence wears out the heart

Missing can be seen as a hole
in the heart, that imaginary
valentine where we store
our emotions.

Absence of someone loved
can be a presence, a lack
that whispers, that raises
hair on your neck

with fear of no return.
Final absence is a black
hole sucking your whole
life into it unless

you thrust it from you
again and again and
again, supper with the plate
solemn as a moon;

two a.m. waking to empty-
ness louder than a shout;
a voice you hear, but
no one is speaking, ever.

A republic of cats

Nobody rules. They all
take turns. I can never
tell who will chase who
playing war over the couch

and chairs, round and
round again until suddenly
they stop as if a whistle
blew in their heads.

Five of them, aged fifteen
to two. Who will curl
together making one cushion
of patchwork fur? Who

will painstakingly lick
a friend, washing and
cuddling. Who will growl
at their friend of last hour?

The one rule is where each
sleeps at night, their spot
in the bed and with whom?
It is written in bone.

What do they expect?

What traces have I left
on all the bodies I have held?
Do they remember my mouth?
Let them forget.

Some come like cats howling
in the night for sex withheld.
Some have gone from my mind.
Their scent has drifted off.

Some I remember with anger
but that too runs down the drain.
Maybe the sink is still dirty.
Maybe the water is clean.

I dream of none of them.
I dream of my mother and cats.
I dream of danger and hunger.
I dream my dying.

What prints do we leave
on old lovers? Do they wash
off or wear down? Sometimes
they turn up expecting

that I will be that girl they
bedded, maybe they still

see her smooth and willing.
They find only me

like an old oak rooted deep,
like a cat who has learned
where to find her food
and where she will only starve.

Decades of intimacy creating

What we weave, day into night into day
now and again, I'm sure looks lumpy
rough burlap from the outside, but
in its house like an oriole's nest
hanging from our sugar maple, we curl
and coil and feed and doze together.

We exchange dreams in the thick
night. We pass tasks between us.
We polish each other's noses
like doorknobs. We crawl into
each other turning round and round
like a cat making a place to sleep.

A long marriage is a quiet epic
full of battles won and lost and ended
by treaties and half forgotten,
of full-throated songs and whispered
treatises, of wispy and rocky promises,
of friendships that dried up like old

apples stored too long and friendships
with cycles of famine and plenty. Cycles
of discovery exploring new islands, cycles
of retreat back into the couple exploring
each other's strange core and familiar
skin, making it new again and again.

We used to be close, I said

I gripped you like a speckled serpent
sinewy, twisting in my tiring arms,
finally breaking free to bite me.

I thought us more alike than we
ever were. In part we invented
each other in a clouded mirror.

We talked, oh long into the night
but did we ever listen? What
did we hear but our wishes?

I gave and you graciously
accepted and then I resented.
When is my turn that never came?

The turning came: the scorpion end
with the poison sting in its tail.
The polychrome egg of our friend-

ship broke open and the rot within
dyed the air mustard yellow. How
long ago that embryo must've died.

A wind suddenly chills you

Unless illness sticks a knife in you
between the ribs like a mugger
from behind, you never imagine
your death until your friends

begin to die. There you are
in a field suddenly stripped bare
with a north wind sandpapering
your skin and when you look

around, where have all the flowers
and bushes and prancing hares
gone? Where are the quick
foxes, the wandering butterflies?

Even your dog at heel has passed
under the soil and rain pours
through him. Then you feel the skull
pressing through your cheeks

as if eager to expose itself
like a flasher in the park.
All the friends, the lovers,
the cats and dogs with whom

you shared rooms and beds—
their memories bloom like ghost
flowers brighter, more vivid
than the remaining weeds that grow.

Why she frightens me

My old cat Malkah howls at night
waking me. Sometimes I'm
kind, get up and bring her
to bed, pet and cuddle.

Sometimes I'm pissed off
chase her from the bedroom
shut the door tight. I wonder
what she is wanting in darkness

when we are all in bed, when
even the other cats sleep.
She is frail, gets two kinds
of medicine daily.

I am not so frisky myself—
arthritis in my knees
from a treadmill accident
in a run-down gym.

I think her howling scares
me because I hear in it
the vault of loneliness old
age threatens to us all.

That I could face not so much
death but years of getting up

in a silent house, pottering
around talking to myself

because there is no one
to care any longer what
I say and so my words
dry up and turn to dust.

My sweetness, my desire

Pumpkin I call you, sweet
and spicy pie. Mango
juicy. Scotch bonnet hot.
Dark chocolate. Espresso.
Fresh squeezed orange
juice thick with pulp.

You come through for
me time after time and
again. Reliable as Old
Faithful. Solid as granite.
You always give me
the gift of laughter.

Whatever I love you try
to love. What threatens me
you stand on guard. We
talk and we talk but it
never wears out. Together
we lay out a feast of love.

They come, they go in the space of a breath

We are told on certain days and nights
the dead are close to us. Yet I find
Shalimar perfume, cinnamon, roasting
chicken can summon them, so that
my grandmother stands just behind me,
my mother sits at my vanity staring
into her vanished face.

If like Orpheus I try to turn to them,
seize their presence, shuffle unanswered
questions before them, cards on a table
faceup, they wisp away like the scent
that brought them. If I think of them,
remembering a dress, a laugh rising
like smoke to the ceiling

they stay away. They come when
they choose and leave so quickly
I wonder if it happened. Sometimes
I hear my mother's voice behind

me, commenting on my cooking,
my clothing. Grandma has come
like Eliyahu on Pesach,

stood for a moment over the laden
table and left again. Two of my cats
came back to visit, ever so briefly.
What do they want, these dead
ones that never linger? They tease,
perhaps, or have only as much energy
as a candle that burns itself out.

In storms I can hear the surf a mile away

You may love the ocean. Never boring,
always in motion, sliding up the shingle
then sucked back in, waves with manes
of white lions' lashing at the shore, waves
standing like a bear tearing at the dunes.

You may love the ocean, but it does
not love you back. It would as soon eat
you as keep you afloat. Perhaps it
loves the great whales, perhaps it
likes walruses, but it's always hungry.

You may love the ocean like my friend
who at eighty will go far out twice
a day if he can get a tourist to pay
his gas. He likes to be out of sight
of land. The sea lurks under his boat

waiting. The ocean is always beautiful
here in all weathers it churns up. It
does not approve of land and wants to
take it back. Someday it will. Even
the hill I live on: sandy bottom.

Tides will stir the ashes of my mother
and the tiny bones of my cats. My grave
will be home to crabs. Who is to say
that is not just that the sea take into
itself what long ago it gave us.

ACKNOWLEDGMENTS

"Made in Detroit," Napalm Health Spa, 2012.

"The frontroom," *Paterson Literary Review*, Vol. 39, 2011–2012.

"Detroit, February 1943," *Third Wednesday*, Vol. 2, Issue 2, Spring 2010.

"Things that will never happen here again," *Poet Lore*, Vol. 108, No. 1/2, Spring/Summer 2013.

"Detroit fauna," *Third Wednesday*, Vol. 3, Issue 2, 2011.

"Family vacation to Yellowstone," "Remnants still visible," "Hard rain and potent thunder," Connotation Press, Congeries with John Hoppenthaler, Vol. II, Issue IV, December 2010.

"The rented lakes of my childhood," *Third Wednesday*, Vol. 5, Issue 3, Summer 2013.

"Thirteen," "By the river of Detroit," *Third Wednesday*, Vol. 3, Issue 2, 2011.

"She held forth," *Paterson Literary Review*, Vol. 39, 2011–2012.

"The scent of apple cake," "Ashes in their places," *San Diego Poetry Annual*, 2012–13.

"City bleeding," "My time in better dresses," *Third Wednesday*, Vol. VIII, No. 1, Winter 2014.

"Mehitabel & me" is forthcoming in *Long Island Sounds Anthology*.

"The street that was," *Fifth Wednesday*, Issue 12, Fall 2012.

"What my mother gave me," "Ashes in their places," *San Diego Poetry Annual*, 2011–12.

"Our neverending entanglement," *The Pinch*, Spring 2012.

"Ashes in their places," *San Diego Poetry Annual*, 2011–12.

"January orders," "We have come through," *The Poetry Porch*, Spring 2013.

"How I gained respect for night herons," *Elohi Gadugi Journal*, Summer 2013.

"The constant exchange," *Cape Cod Poetry Review*, Vol. II, Winter 2014.

"May opens wide," Poetsusa.com, 2012.

"Wisteria can pull a house down," "The suicide of dolphins," *Atlanta Review*, Spring/Summer, Vol. XX, Issue 2.

"June 15th, 8 p.m.," *San Pedro River Review*, Special Issue: Harbors and Harbor Towns, Summer 2013.

"Ignorance bigger than the moon," "Even if we try not to let go," Ibbetson Street Press, No. 4, December 2013.

"Little house with no door," *Broadkill Review*, Vol. 7, Issue 4, July/August 2013.

"Why did the palace of excess have cockroaches?" *Haibun Today*, Vol. 7, No. 3, September 2013.

"There were no mountains in Detroit," *Haibun Today*, Vol. 7, No. 11, December 2014.

"But soon there will be none," *Paterson Literary Review*, Issue 42, 2014–15.

"Missing, missed," *Haibun Today*, Vol. 8, No. 3, September 2014.

"Death's charming face," *Spillway*, Issue 19, Fall 2012.

"The frost moon," *Ibbetson Street*, No. 31, Summer 2012.

"December arrives like an unpaid bill," *Red Thread, Gold Thread*, Vol. 2, 2012.

"The poor are no longer with us," "These bills are long unpaid," *Monthly Review,* Vol. 64, No. 1, May 2012.

"Don't send dead flowers," *Revolution House,* Vol. 2.1, April 2012.

"A hundred years since the Triangle Fire," *Monthly Review,* Vol. 62, Issue 11, 2011.

"Ethics for Republicans," *On the Issues Magazine,* Winter 2012.

"Another obituary," *Ms. Magazine,* April 2012.

"What it means," *Monthly Review,* Vol. 64, No. 4, September 2012.

"How have the mighty . . ." *Tryst,* October 2010.

"We know," EcoPoetry.org, November 2013.

"The passion of a fan," *Literary Arts Annual,* 2013.

"In pieces," *So It Goes: The Literary Journal of the Kurt Vonnegut Memorial Library,* 2013.

"Ghosts," *Monthly Review,* Vol. 65, March 2013.

"One of the expendables," *Cape Cod Times,* May 28, 2013.

"Let's meet in a restaurant," *Visions International,* Winter 2014.

"Come fly without me," *Ibbetson Street,* No. 28, November 2010.

"Hope is a long, slow thing," *The Progressive,* Vol. 76, No. 12/1, December 2012/January 2013.

"The late year," *Midstream,* September/October 2002.

"Erev New Years," *Midstream,* Summer 2011.

"Head of the year," The '98 Lunar Calendar, September 1998.

"Late that afternoon they come," *Midstream,* Vol. 58, Summer 2012.

"The wall of cold descends," *Spillway,* Issue 19, Fall 2012.

"How she learned," *Prism, Journal for Holocaust Educators,* Vol. 3, Spring 2011.

"Working at it," *Jewish Women's Literary Annual,* Vol. 9, 2013.

"The order of the seder," *Midstream,* Vol. 50, No. 3, April 2004.

"The two cities," *Tikkun,* Israel at 60, May/June 2008.

"Where silence waits," *Moment,* 2011.

"I say Kaddish but still mourn," *Poetica Magazine,* Summer 2012.

"Little diurnal tragedies," *Sugar Mule,* Issue 39, November 2011.

"The next evolutionary step," *New Guard Literary Review,* Vol. III, 2014.

"That was Cobb Farm," *december* magazine, Vol. 25.2, Fall/Winter 2014.

"They meet," *Third Wednesday,* Winter 2013.

"A cigarette left smoldering," *Potomac Review,* 2013.

"Discovery motion," "Different voices, one sentence," *Softblow,* January 2012.

"Sun in January," *Muddy River Poetry Review,* Fall 2013.

"Little rabbit's dream song," "Cotton's wife," *Ibbetson Street,* No. 31, Summer 2012.

"That summer day," *The Mas Tequila Review,* Issue 5, Fall 2012.

"Insomniac prayer at 2 a.m.," *Poetry Porch,* 2014.

"The body in the hot tub," *San Diego Poetry Annual,* 2011–12.

"Looking back in utter confusion," "What do they expect?" *Superstition Review,* Issue 9, 2012.

"In the Peloponnesus one April afternoon," *Green Mountain Review,* Vol. 24, No. 1, 2011.

"The end not yet in sight," *The San Pedro River Review,* Vol. 4, No. 5, Fall 2012.

"Loving clandestinely," "We used to be close, I said," *Marsh Hawk Review,* Spring 2014.

"The visible and the in-," *New Mirage Journal*, 2011.

"What's left" (published as "What remains"), *Contemporary World Literature*, Vol. 4, Spring 2011.

"Corner of Putnam and Pearl," *San Pedro River Review*, Vol. 5, No. 1, Spring 2013.

"Bang, crash over," *Blue Lyra Review*, July 2012.

"Sins of omission," *Calyx*, Vol. 19, No. 1, Winter 1999–2000.

"Even if we try not to let go," *december* magazine, Vol. 24, 2013.

"Marinade for an elderly rabbit," *5 AM*, Issue 35, Summer 2012.

"Contemplating my breasts," *Muddy River Poetry Review*, Fall 2013.

"Words hard as stones," *Marsh Hawk Review*, Fall 2010.

"Absence wears out the heart," *Paterson Literary Review*, Issue 42, 2014–15.

"A republic of cats," *Contemporary World Literature*, Vol. 4, Spring 2011.

"Decades of intimacy creating," *Third Wednesday*, Spring 2013.

"A wind suddenly chills you," *A Gathering of the Tribes*, Issue 13, 2011.

"Why she frightens me," *Paterson Literary Review*, Issue 41, 2013–14.

"My sweetness, my desire," *Broadkill Review*, Vol. 8, Issue 5, Fall 2014.

"They come, they go in the space of a breath," *Paterson Literary Review*, No. 42, 2014.

"In storms I can hear the surf a mile away," *Paterson Literary Review*, Issue 43, 2015–16.

A NOTE ABOUT THE AUTHOR

Marge Piercy is the author of eighteen previous poetry collections, seventeen novels and a book of short stories, four nonfiction books, two memoirs and one play. Her work has been translated into nineteen languages, and she has won many honors, including the Golden Rose, the oldest poetry award in the country. She lives on Cape Cod with her husband, Ira Wood, the novelist, memoirist, community radio interviewer, and essayist. She has given more than five hundred readings and lectures in the United States and abroad.

A NOTE ON THE TYPE

This book was set in Scala, a typeface designed by the Dutch designer Martin Majoor (b. 1960) in 1988 and released by the FontFont foundry in 1990. While designed as a fully modern family of fonts containing both a serif and a sans serif alphabet, Scala retains many refinements normally associated with traditional fonts.

Typeset by Scribe,
Philadelphia, Pennsylvania

Printed and bound by Thomson-Shore,
Dexter, Michigan

Designed by Soonyoung Kwon

mL   5-16